Locks & No Bagels!
A Kid's Guide To The Panama Canal

Photography by John D. Weigand
Poetry by Penelope Dyan

Bellissima Publishing, LLC
Jamul, California
www.bellissimapublishing.com

Copyright © 2019 by Penny D. Weigand & John D. Weigand

All rights reserved. No part of this book may be
reproduced or transmitted in any form or by any means,
electronic or mechanical, including photocopying,
recording, or by any other means, or by any information or
storage retrieval system, without permission from the publisher.

ISBN 978-1-61477-386-3
First Edition

"You might not get bagels with these locks, but you will get an eye full!"

PENELOPE DYAN

Locks & No Bagels!
Bellissima Publishing, LLC

Introduction

The Panama Canal, a man-made waterway in Panama, connects the Atlantic Ocean with the Pacific Ocean. It cuts across the Isthmus of Panama, serving maritime trade. The canal locks at each end actually lift ships up to Gatun Lake, a man-made lake that was created to lessen the excavation work on the canal. Building the Panama Canal was a dangerous endeavor, and seeing the project through to its completion is a tribute to perseverance. France began building the canal in 1881, and the United States took over the project in 1904 and opened the canal on August 15, 1914. There were many perils during the years that transpired, but this book isn't about that!

This 'learn to read' book is meant to show the Panama Canal the way a kid would see it, and enjoy it, with its ups and downs! And as a kid travels through the pages of this book, he or she can also practice reading skills through the author's clever use of word recognition and word repetition and rhyme. When a kid is all finished going through the Panama Canal through this book's pages, they can go to the Bellissimavideo YouTube channel and watch the free music video that goes along with this book; and they can see even more of the Panama Canal!

Locks & No Bagels!
Bellissima Publishing, LLC

Locks & No Bagels!
A Kid's Guide To The Panama Canal

Photography by John D. Weigand
Poetry by Penelope Dyan

Your ship goes up, and it does down;
and it gives you a chance
to see what you see,
as you look all around.
Mom looks over at the ship deck clock.
Dad looks anxious.
Dad's camera is ready
as you approach the first lock!

Dad explains,
"Each ship MUST get in line.
We'll go right straight through the lock
when it's OUR ship's turn AND time!"

Another cruise ship enters the lock.
Mom looks AGAIN
at the ship deck clock.

There are wheels on the canal sides!
And Dad tells Sis AND you,
"The wheels on the sides of the canal help roll ALL the boats through!"
Mom laughs and says,
"This isn't a BUS!
This happen to be a boat!
And we don't actually ROLL, because we actually FLOAT!"
Dad says,
"Well, last night I did feel this boat rock AND roll!
So maybe this boat has a musical soul!"

You see one dinghy.
And then you count two.
You suppose the two dinghies
have an important job
they must do!

Then you see a giant black crane;
and Dad jokingly says,
"Haven't you heard?
A crane can ALSO be a kind of a bird!"
Mom shakes her head.
She doesn't think Dad is funny.
So she changes the subject;
and she says,
"I'm so glad TODAY is sunny!"

You get to the first lock,
and the first lock opens wide.
Sis complains, shakes her head,
and loudly grumbles,
"I want to go back inside!"

Equipment and machinery travel,
going up and down a track!
Dad exclaims,
"It's way, way too late NOW!
AND we're just NOT going back!"
You think about
all of the sweat and tears,
AND about how
building the Panama Canal
took so many LONG and perilous years!

You see some men working.
Then Dad tells you something more.
Dad says.
"The Panama Canal connects
the Atlantic Ocean to the Pacific Ocean,
so goods can travel shore to shore."
And then Mom adds,
". . . AND it connects people too!"
And Sis grumbles,
"I wish there was something ELSE
that we could do!"
But (after all) Sis is VERY young.
She doesn't yet realize
learning about accomplishment is fun!

You shout VERY, VERY loudly!
(Everyone looks.)
You shout
"I see a crane
with two brightly colored orange hooks!"
Sis, I am afraid, ISN'T impressed.
Mom says she'll take Sis inside now,
because Sis NEEDS a little rest.

Then the locks open again.
You look down . . . as into new waters
you begin to carefully wend . . .
well . . . not YOU exactly, but
(ACTUALLY) the boat . . .
on which everyone aboard this craft,
through THIS lock,
will now sail and float!

And then you see a BIG cargo ship,
being pulled by ropes straight ahead;
and you think all about this day,
when you LATER go to bed.
You think about the ALL of the courage
AND about ALL of the strife,
how some men so VERY long ago worked
so HARD for a BETTER way of life!
And THEN you think all about the moon.
You wonder if men will be connecting
entire galaxies someday VERY soon!
You wonder if someday you will sail away,
and if you will sail right smack through
the Milky Way!

"Everything comes and goes,
especially on the Panama Canal!"

PENELOPE DYAN

www.ingramcontent.com/pod-product-compliance
Ingram Content Group UK Ltd.
Pitfield, Milton Keynes, MK11 3LW, UK
UKHW060133240426
12048UKWH00002B/24